"Move over Snoopy. Pavlov is the funniest dog I have ever seen . . . he and his owner have more adventures in hilarity than should be legal."

—Ocala (Fla.) Star-Banner

"Martin's humor is as hilariously playful as his drawings and it's no wonder that he has developed a worldwide following."

—Pasadena Star-News

PAVLOV'S PAD

Ted Martin

TOR
TOM DOHERTY ASSOCIATES

PAVLOV'S PAD

Copyright © 1982, 1984

Many of the cartoons in this book have appeared in *Pavlov's Pad* published in 1982 by Andrews and McMeel, Inc.

All rights reserved. Printed in the United States of America. No part of this book may be used or reproduced in any manner whatsoever without written permission except in the case of reprints in the context of reviews. For information write Andrews and McMeel, Inc., a Universal Press Syndicate Company, 4400 Johnson Drive, Fairway, Kansas 66205.

ISBN: 0-440-06854-1

Published by
Dell Publishing Co., Inc.
1 Dag Hammarskjold Plaza
New York, New York 10017

Dell ® TM 681510, Dell Publishing Co., Inc.

Printed in the United States of America

First printing—August 1984

"Ready?"

"I can't wait to see the painting you're doing of the car."

"Something seems to tell me I forgot to give you your allowance."

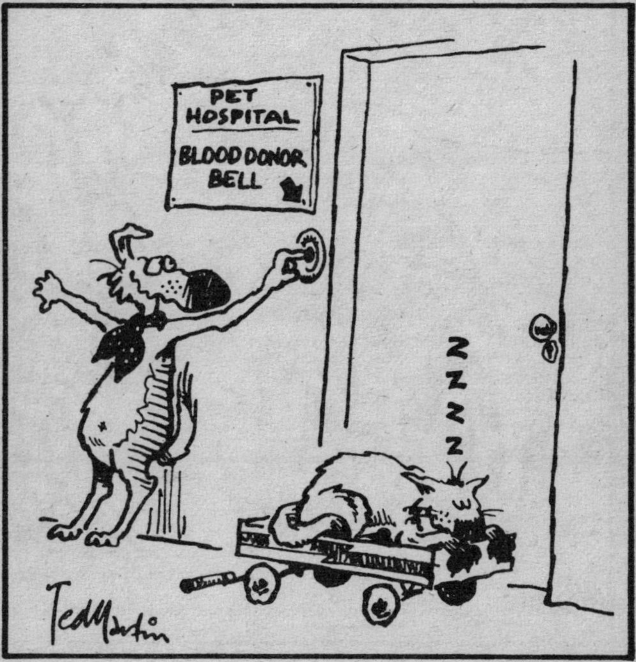
PET HOSPITAL
BLOOD DONOR BELL
Z Z Z Z
Ted Martin

"Mother's not going to be pleased when she finds out you've used masking tape instead of meat skewers."

"No, I will not help you onto the roof with that thing."

"I'm missing my permanent black marker."

"Put that away or I'll set my vicious, man-eating dog on you . . ."

"Pavlov, I know you're in the attic so you can't scare me . . ."

"The neighbors won't get out of our pool, Pavlov — you know the plan . . ."

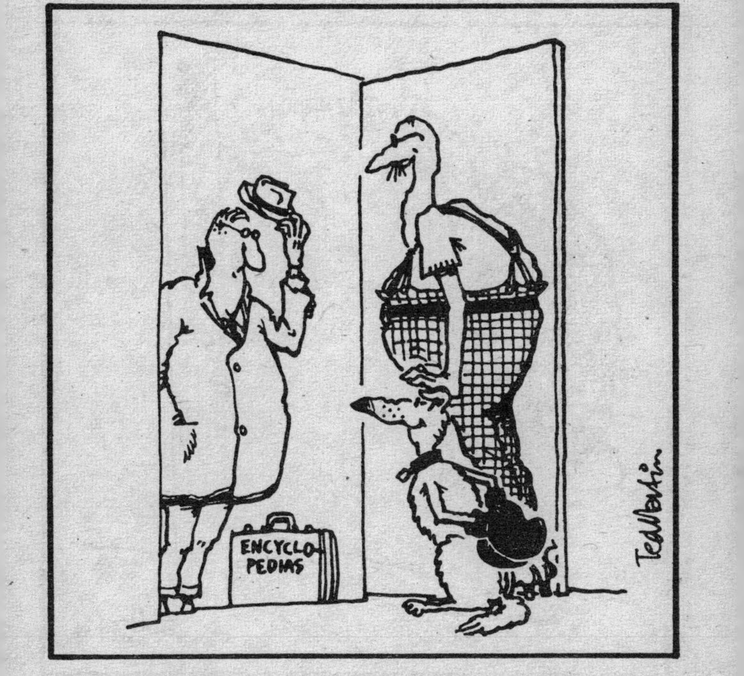
ENCYCLOPEDIAS
TedMartin

"Come on in — he won't bite."

"I don't know any password!"

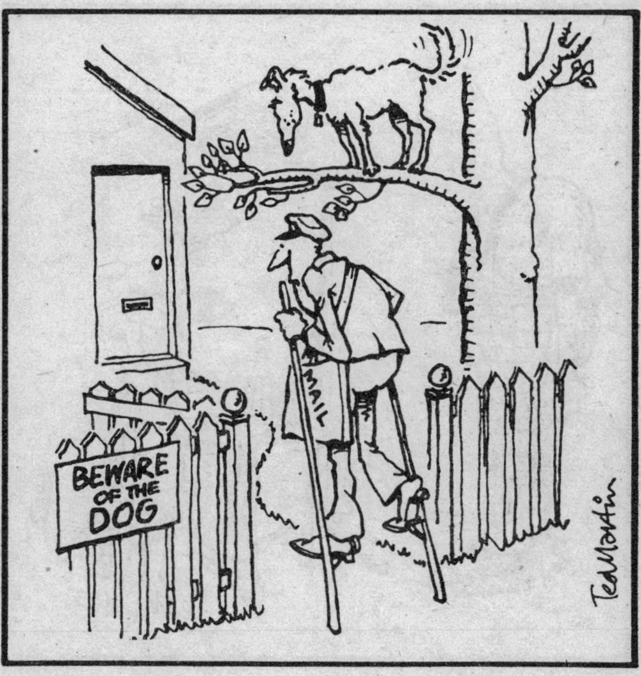
MAIL
BEWARE OF THE DOG
Ted Martin

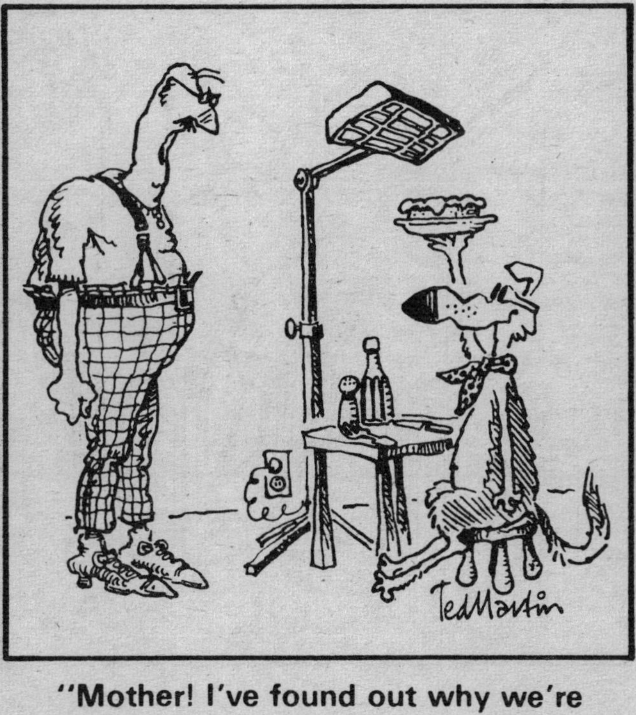
TedMartin

"Mother! I've found out why we're getting grilled cheese on the sunlamp."

"One size-four right-foot sneaker, please."

"I didn't know radio-controlled boats had crews."

"Better hide that walkie-talkie. You've got a 747 taxiing up the driveway."

"That's nothing — wait 'til you taste his coffee."

"You didn't tell me you were going on a picnic."

"You can share my bath, but no dumb wind-up toys, OK?"

"That 17th century treasure map you sold me — check if I'm digging next to the correct telephone pole."

"I took it away from him before he could do any damage."

"He's auditioning the cat for his ice-show act — you're next."

"Cool it. It's the Joneses. They've canceled their dinner date."

"It's so lifelike, I could swear it moved . . ."

"Don't forget which pile of sand Father's under — he's got the car keys."

"You trying to figure out who put Crazy Glue on your scratching post?"

"Only you could think of something like that."

"The back door's wide open."

"How am I supposed to know the sign means what it says? . . ."

"His new superscreen TV has blown a fuse. Can he plug it in here?"

"It's not a spelling mistake. Clem was one of the goldfish."

"I thought he was stargazing."

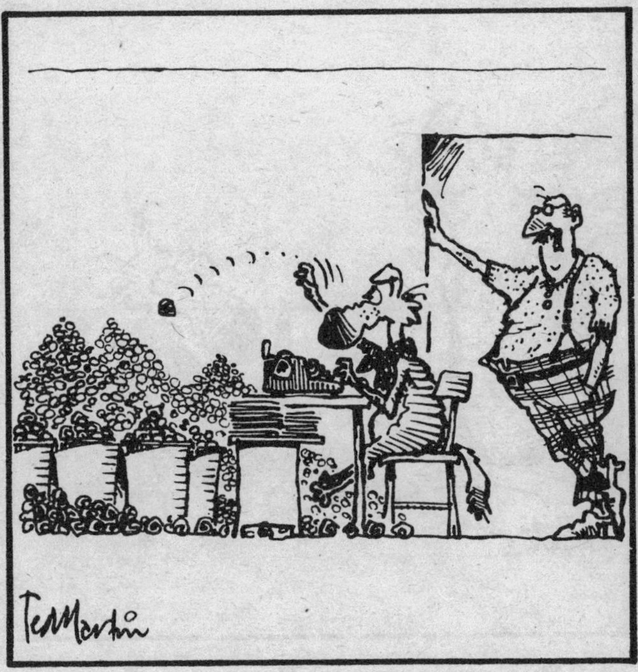
TedMartin

"How's the novel coming?"

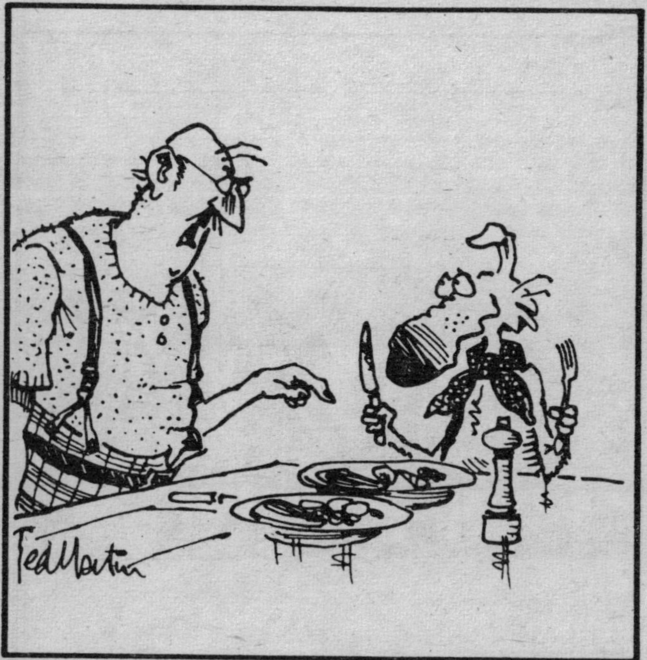
Ted Martin

"This one's yours. The peas aren't touching the carrots, the meat's not touching the potatoes and the gravy's only on the meat, OK?"

"Mother, remember that old home-perm you asked Pavlov to throw in the garbage?"

"Ain't that dog something to be proud of — practicing instead of watching TV?"

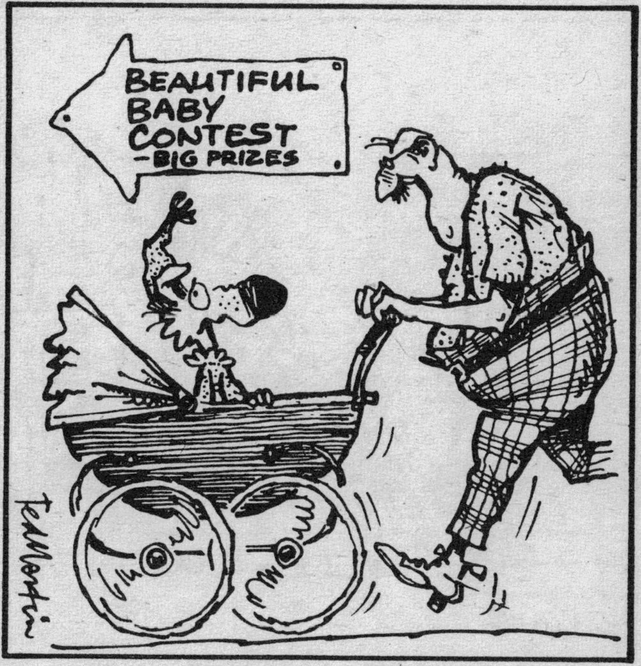
BEAUTIFUL
BABY
CONTEST
-BIG PRIZES

"Don't forget, it's a 50/50 split."

"Wasn't it your shoes that needed polishing?"

"I don't believe it, we're going through 50 ft. of dental floss a day"

"Here kitty kitty, here kitty kitty . . ."

"I'd be really grateful if you could add more hair and thin me down a bit."

"Mother was thinking of taking me out to dinner if she could find her wig and high heels."

"Couldn't I just have an order of dry toast?"

". . . and stay clear of the wallpaper until it's dry."

"I'll break the news gently to Mother that you're making her a charm bracelet."

"Can he play through?"

"Pavlov wants to know what else he can do to help out now that he's pruned your roses."

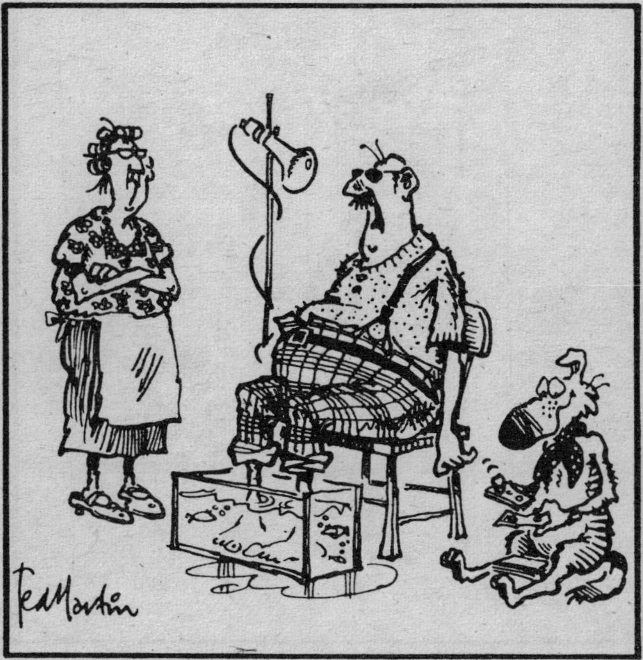
Ted Martin

"He conned me into buying a 'sea-and-sun' package."

"Dog? What dog? I don't own a dog."

"Couldn't find his Davy Crockett hunting hat anywhere."

"Can't you think of an easier way to trim your toenails?"

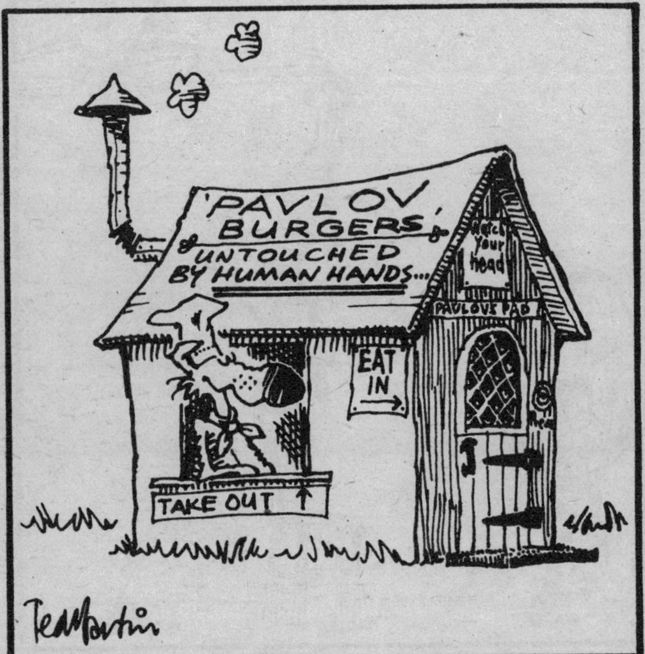
'PAVLOV BURGERS'
UNTOUCHED BY HUMAN HANDS...
Watch your head
PAVLOV'S PAD
EAT IN
TAKE OUT
TedMartin

"He found your mother's homemade chili recipe."

"Come back — that's not a pull-toy."

"I can't see how that fish is gonna help get your chimney cleaned."

"What are you doing back there with your spaghetti?"

"He's right, y'know. It says Frozen Fish on the menu and that's what he's serving."

"Well, whadayou want?"

"Show me something that says the captain must go down with his ship."

"Great fish chowder — where d'ya get the fish from?"

"The deeper you dig, the more chance you've got of growing a prize winner."

"Wanna add a line to mother's letter telling her how much we miss her?"

"Pay attention here. Your next math problem is concerned with moving a recumbent mass of energy."

"Hold it. That's not the way to make them oven-ready."

"The idea was to do that before you filled the pool."

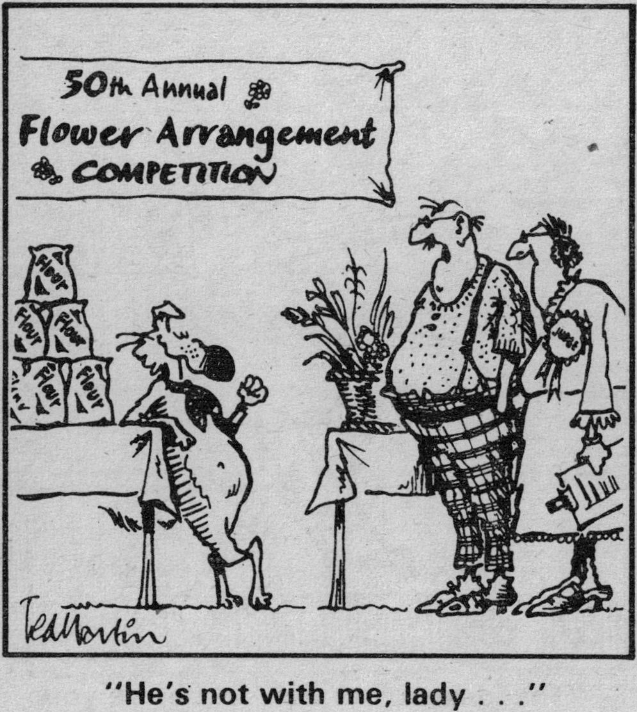
50th Annual
Flower Arrangement
COMPETITION
FLOUR
FLOUR
FLOUR
FLOUR
FLOUR
JUDGE

"He's not with me, lady . . ."

"That suntan oil sure has an appetizing aroma."

"What kind of a scam is this? These are chicken ribs."

"I remembered what it was we left off the grocery list."

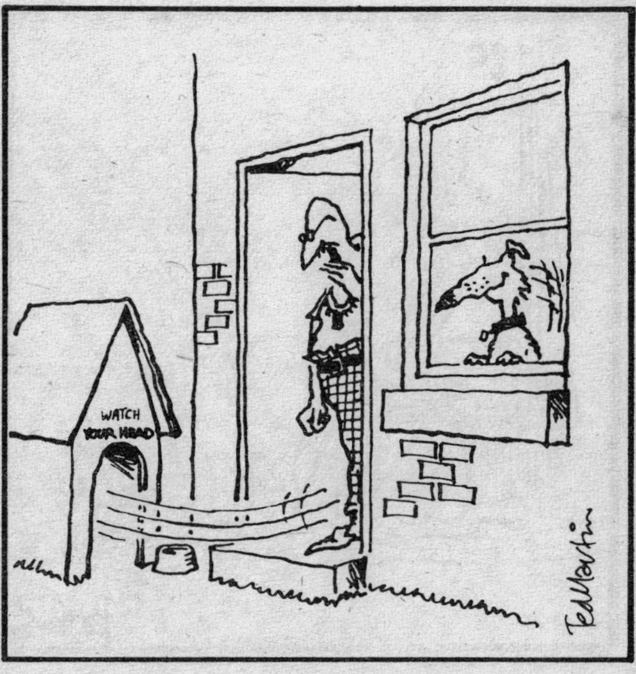
WATCH
YOUR HEAD

"You can come in for five . . ."

"Be patient and stop shivering. All we need is a good breeze."

"He doesn't use a lot of soap..."

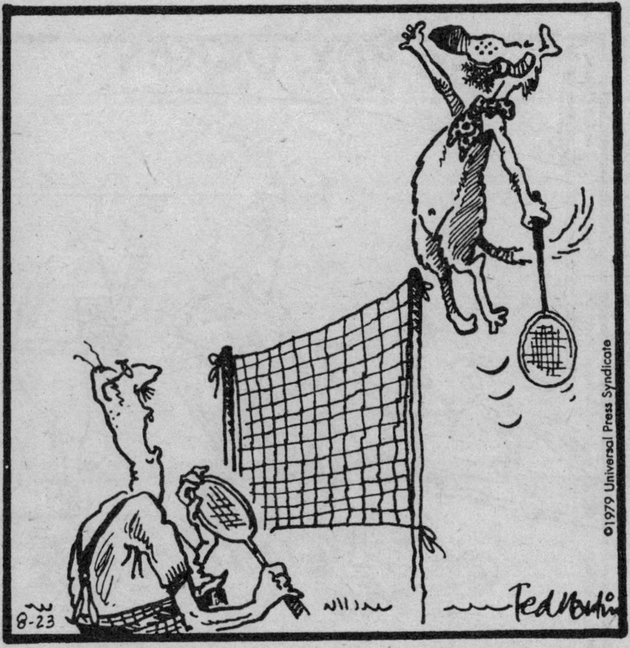
©1979 Universal Press Syndicate
8-23

"OK! So your pappy was a retriever."

"I am about to enhance the flavor of the baked salmon with this fantastic sauce..."

"The chocolate cake isn't on top of the fridge anymore."

"What was it you wanted a wrench for?"

"I thought you only took the studio tour?"

"Ten days without food and I haven't lost an ounce?"

TedMartin
12-19
©1980 Universal Press Syndicate

"That's not the channel changer!"

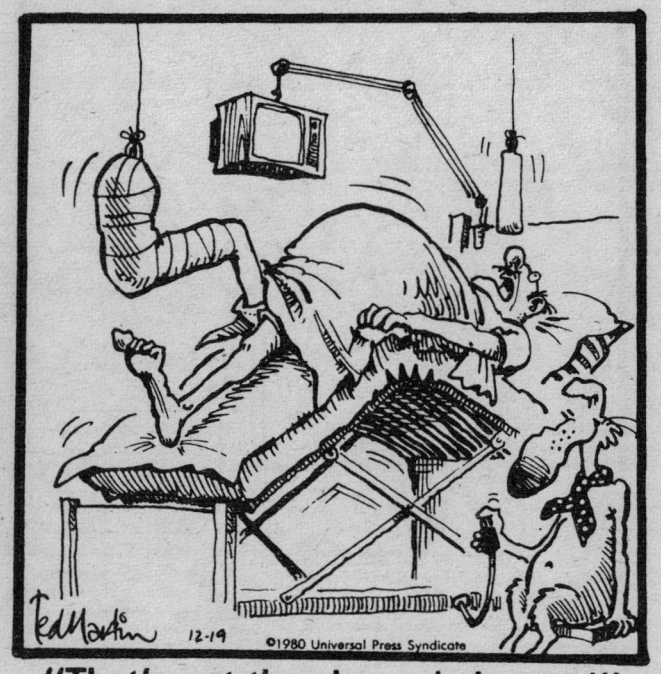

"Not too kind now; he's turning blue."

"Every time we get to the line 'By the light of the silvery moon,' some turkey starts to howl."

"When he starts his upswing, that's your cue."

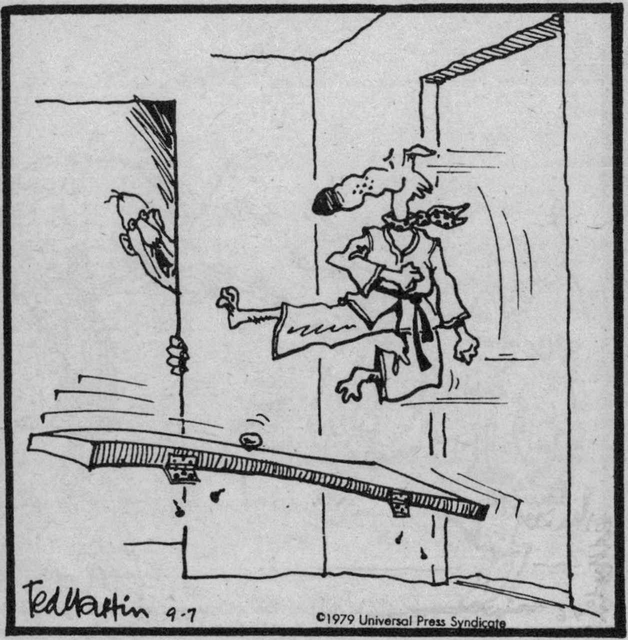

TedMartin 9-7
©1979 Universal Press Syndicate

"Sorry, I didn't hear the doorbell."

"Couldn't you practice with spoons?"

"He won't bother you. I told him you were a dog food salesman."

"Everybody knows what it means:
I heart New York."

"Oh, come on. I'm not ordering a Shirley Temple for nobody."

"Wanna throw another log on, Pavlov?"

"Are you sure you haven't traveled this way before?"

"Let Pavlov out. I think he wants to bark."

"I know it's late, but scene 56 calls for you to bring me a cream pie."

"We'd make a few bucks more if you'd only thumb a ride back."

"Rule No. 1 is: Wait until after class before chewing garlic."

"Ignore the vacuum cleaning part; this is rug shampoo."

"He's here to try out for the part of Orphan Annie's dog."

"Keep that cold to yourself. You'll find tissues in the caboose, OK?"

"OK, so I forgot the little light had busted."

"When I'm through, the bone's yours, OK?"

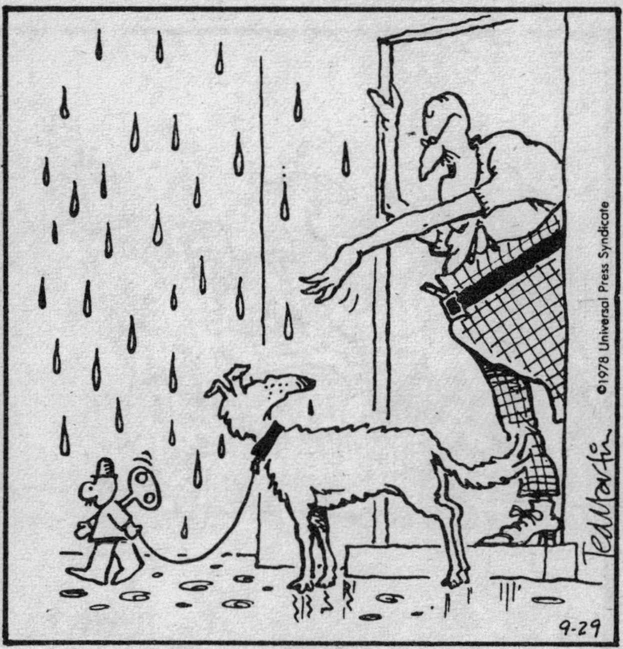
©1978 Universal Press Syndicate
TedMartin
9-29

"Go on, Pavlov. Go walkies."

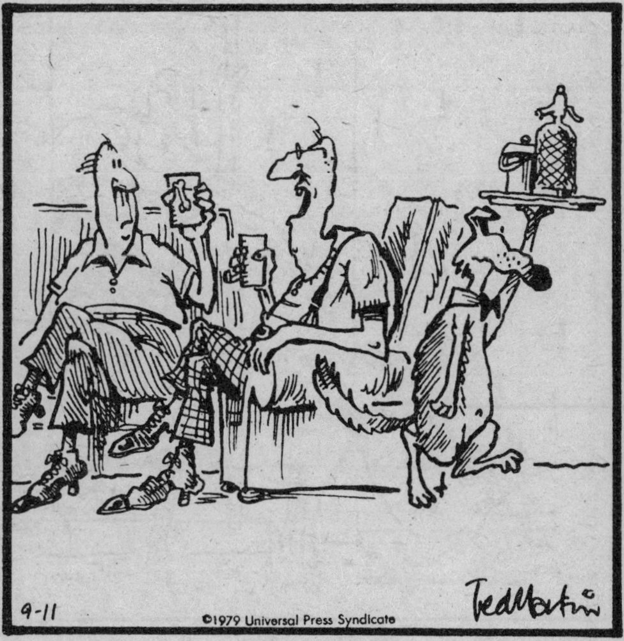
9-11
©1979 Universal Press Syndicate
TedMartin

"Excuse the dog biscuit-shaped ice—but you know how hard it is to get help these days."

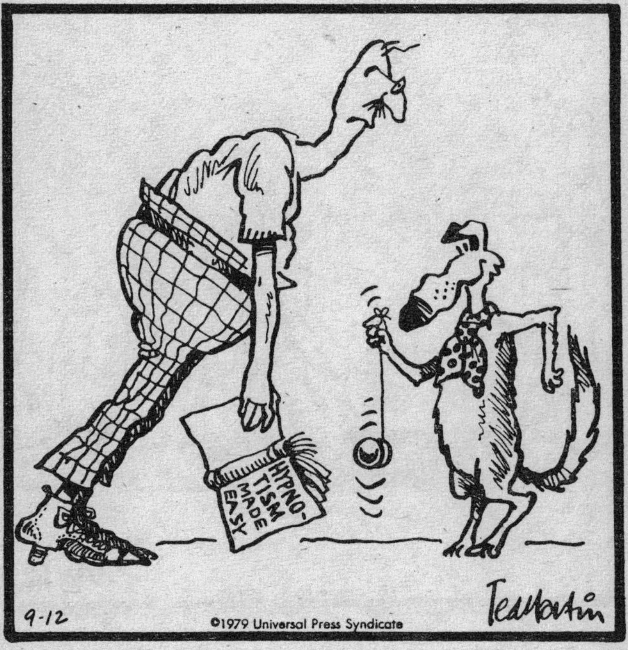
HYPNO-TISM MADE EASY
9-12
©1979 Universal Press Syndicate
TedMartin

"You can quit looking for the back-scratcher."

"But I only want change for a quarter."

"Hold it! When I said 'vet' I was talking about Uncle Willie the veteran."

"What's this—a request for a medley from 'Saturday Night Fever'?"

"You'll have to speak up, doctor, it's the foot-in-the-ear problem again..."

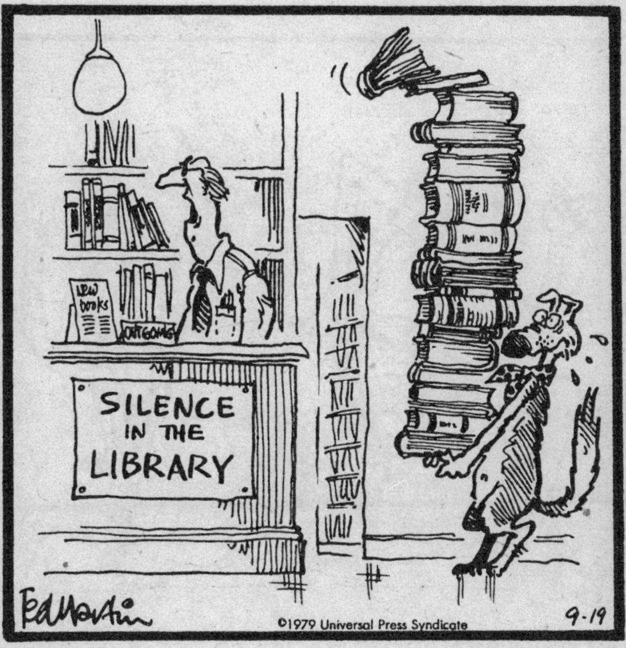
NEW BOOKS
OUTGOING
SILENCE IN THE LIBRARY
©1979 Universal Press Syndicate
9-19

"Who yelled 'timber'?"

"I'm gonna have to quit jogging with you. I've got a thumping noise in my ears."

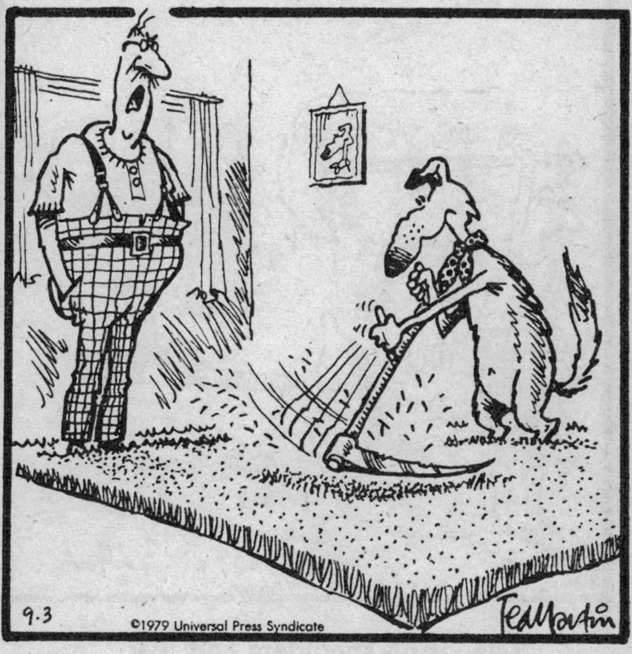
9·3
©1979 Universal Press Syndicate
TedMartin

"Lose a contact lens?"

"Canoes on shoulders and ready to portage!"

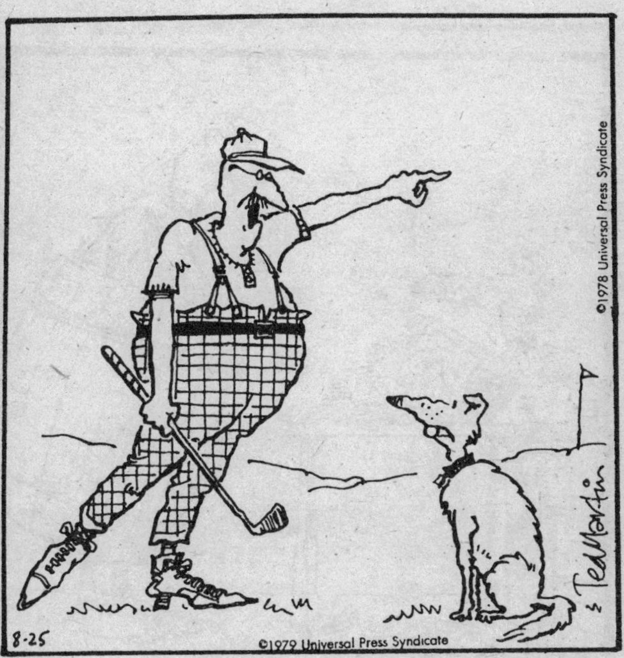
©1978 Universal Press Syndicate
TedMartin
8-25
©1979 Universal Press Syndicate

"To the flag, Pavlov."

"How about double or nothing?"

"I'm not so sure that's how one starts to make an omelet."

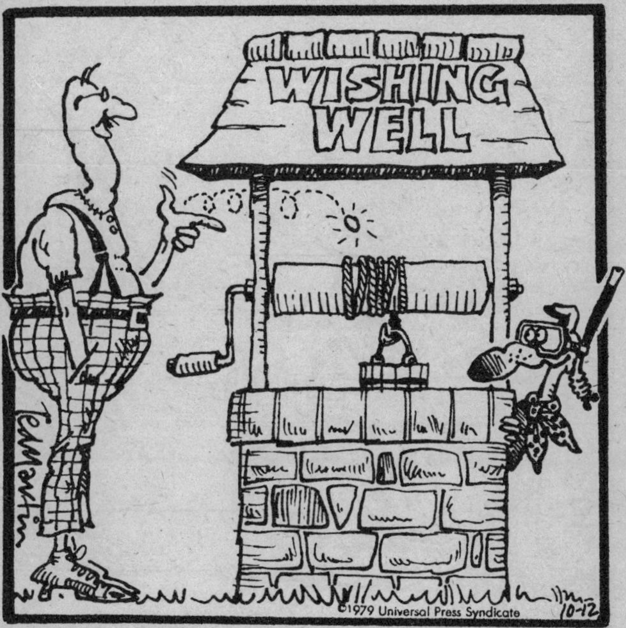

WISHING WELL
TedMartin
©1979 Universal Press Syndicate
10-12

"And don't forget, this is touch football—
no tackling!"

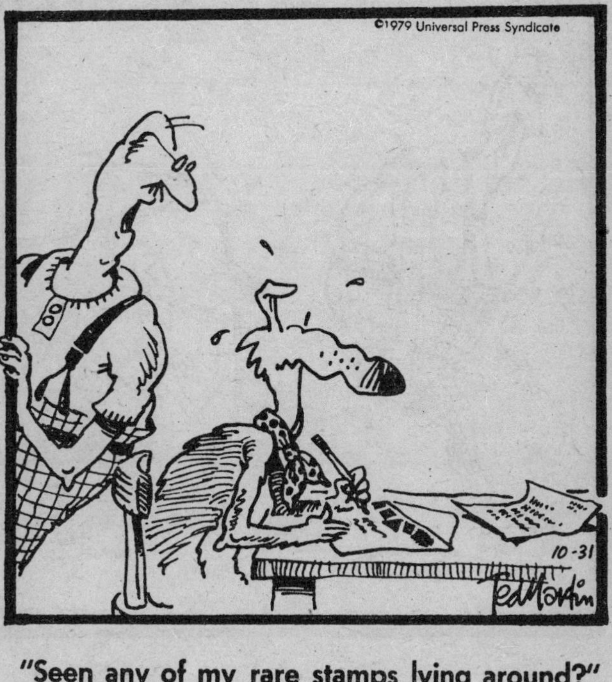
©1979 Universal Press Syndicate
10-31

"Seen any of my rare stamps lying around?"

"How much longer before you hand in your thesis?"

"Forget his dessert. He just ate your candle."

"Didn't we have an understanding this was a solo act...?"

"If he's not a dalmatian, you've got problems."